Girl Talk

Tangles, Growth Spurts, and Being You

Questions and Answers About Growing Up

by Nancy Loewen and Paula Skelley
illustrated by Julissa Mora

Content adviser:
John E. Desrochers, PhD

CAPSTONE PRESS
a capstone imprint

Table of Contents

Isabella   Lan   Claudia   Sagal

What's the best part of growing up?

Is it that you get to do more things on your own? That your allowance gets bigger? That you start looking less like a little kid and more like an adult?

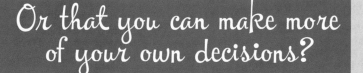

Or that you can make more of your own decisions?

For all the great parts of growing up, there are just as many confusing parts. **GROWING UP IS ABOUT CHANGE—LOTS OF IT!**

One day you're playing dress up, and the next you're wearing a bra. Your moods are all over the place, and sometimes you wish everybody would just **LEAVE YOU ALONE.**

It's normal to have a ton of questions about all the changes you're going through.

That's why we're here—

to give you the info you need to make growing up a little easier. But don't just take OUR advice. Be sure to talk to your parents. After all, they were kids once too. Teachers, counselors, relatives, and other trusted adults can help as well.

Q I've been hearing the word "puberty" a lot lately. What does puberty mean?

A Puberty is when your body begins to change from child to adult. For girls that means your breasts will start to develop, and hair will grow under your arms and in your pubic area. You'll get taller. Your body will start to fill out and change shape. And you'll start getting your period.

Puberty doesn't happen all at once. It takes place over a number of years. Some girls start puberty at 8 or 9. Others are 12 or older. Every girl has her own timeline. Your body will know when it's the right time for you.

Q What is B.O.?

A B.O. stands for body odor.

You've heard of hormones, right? Hormones basically tell the body what to do. Hormones also make your sweat glands go a little crazy—especially the ones under your arms. The sweat mixes with bacteria, and that's where the smell comes from.

You can avoid B.O. by taking a bath or shower every day. If you play sports or are just really active, you might even need to bathe twice. You should also use deodorant or antiperspirant. What's the difference? Antiperspirant keeps you from producing sweat, while deodorant battles the bacteria. (Most antiperspirants include a little deodorant too—just in case.)

4

My mom has never talked to me about puberty. How do I get up the courage to ask her questions?

It's hard to talk about this stuff, especially if your mom hasn't brought it up yet. Instead of sitting down for a big formal talk, ask questions while you're doing other things. Some kids and parents have good talks in the car. After a while you'll both get used to the idea that you're old enough to ask these questions. Your conversations should get easier. But if not, it's OK to talk to another trusted adult.

Tip Clip

Some kids put on weight right before a growth spurt. Not a big deal. Eat healthy, sleep well, and the rest will take care of itself.

Some of my friends wear bras, but I'm nowhere near being ready for one. Should I get one anyway?

That's up to you. Some girls can't wait to wear a bra. Others want to put it off as long as they can. You could try one and see what you think. There are cotton bras that feel like T-shirts, which might be a good way to get started. Maybe some days you wear a bra and some days you don't! It's your body and your decision.

My friend looks like she needs to wear a bra. Should I say something?

There's a good chance your friend already knows she needs to wear a bra. Maybe she's embarrassed to talk to an adult about it. Have a friend-to-friend talk and find out what she's thinking.

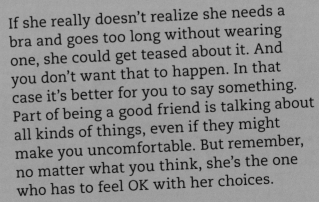

If she really doesn't realize she needs a bra and goes too long without wearing one, she could get teased about it. And you don't want that to happen. In that case it's better for you to say something. Part of being a good friend is talking about all kinds of things, even if they might make you uncomfortable. But remember, no matter what you think, she's the one who has to feel OK with her choices.

Q A few of the boys in my class tease the girls who wear bras, including me. It's so embarrassing. What should we do?

A Don't be embarrassed. The changes you and your girlfriends are going through happen to everyone eventually. Ignore the boys. If they don't stop, tell your teacher. He or she can help sort it out.

The boys themselves may be uncomfortable about growing up. Teasing you might be a way of trying to cover up their feelings. That's not an excuse, though.

Q My dad and I can talk about almost anything, but I'm worried about talking to him about bras and stuff like that.

A Your dad might be more nervous than you are! Both of you are changing. You're the one growing up, but your dad has new challenges as a parent too. You're lucky, because you already have a good relationship with him. If you both get a little embarrassed, that's OK. It will get easier each time you talk.

Q How old do you have to be to shave your legs?

A That depends on how old you are when you WANT to shave your legs, and when your parents say it's OK. Shaving your legs is a choice. Not everyone does. In some countries, women don't shave at all.

Maybe you've heard that your hair will grow back thicker and darker. It won't. It just looks that way because you're seeing the blunt ends of the hair.

Q Help! There's hair growing in my armpits—and other places too. What am I supposed to do about it?

A Hair happens! It's a natural part of growing up.

You don't have to do anything about underarm hair if you don't want to. But if you'd rather go smooth than fuzzy under your arms, you can remove the hair. There are a few ways to do that: shaving, lotions that dissolve hair, and waxing. Each method has its pros and cons. Talk to your mom or another adult you trust. Before you actually try anything, be sure you have a parent's permission.

Q Shaving under my arms scares me. What if I cut myself?

A Shaving can be a little scary at first. But don't worry. If you do cut yourself, it will just sting a little, and the cut will heal quickly.

There are a lot of things you can do to prevent cuts. First, pick a razor that's specially designed to prevent nicks and cuts. Use plenty of soap or shaving cream. Don't press too hard, and rinse the razor often.

If you use an electric razor, the blades won't ever touch your skin directly. Electric razors don't shave as closely as other razors do, but you for sure won't cut yourself.

9

Q I've grown 3 inches this year and wear a bra. Everything about my body seems different and strange. I wish I could go back in time and just be a kid again.

A A lot of girls feel this way. One day you're carefree and confident, and the next day you're tripping over your own feet. It's so confusing! But hang in there. The main thing is to accept yourself as you are, right now. You may feel awkward for a while, but in time you'll get used to the new you.

And you don't have to change the way you act just because your body is different. If you want to snuggle up next to your mom, go ahead. If you feel like watching a scary movie with friends, that's OK too.

The girls on my bus sometimes whisper about "periods." I know they don't mean the little dot at the end of a sentence! Where can I go to get the right information about periods?

 You're smart to ask about the RIGHT information. Sometimes kids don't get all their facts straight, and they spread all sorts of wild ideas. First step: Talk to your mom or another woman you know well. Some of the information gets a little technical, so it's OK to do some research at the library. If there's anything you don't understand, ask an adult to explain it.

Tip Clip

Keep a travel-size deodorant in your backpack. If you forget to put on deodorant at home in the morning, you'll be covered!

Hair and Skin Care

Q My mom wants me to cut my hair. I don't want to. Ever! Why can't I just let it grow?

A Long hair can be so pretty. But even long hair needs a little TLC to keep it healthy. Get a trim at least once every few months to avoid split ends.

Tell your mom why you like your hair long. Then ask why she wants you to cut it. Do you have trouble taking care of your long hair? Does it get in the way when you play sports? Try to find a compromise that works for both of you.

Q I need to wash my hair a lot more often than I used to. It gets greasy so fast! What's going on?

A Greasy hair is no fun. But it's part of growing up. Here's what's going on: At the base of every hair is a tiny oil gland. We need a little oil to keep our hair from getting too dry and breaking. But during puberty, our oil glands sometimes go overboard and make too much oil. That's why you need to wash your hair more often. So keep the shampoo bottle handy.

Q What causes pimples? And how do I keep from getting them?

A Pimples are the worst! But almost every kid gets them at some point. Adults can get them too.

Pimples form when pores (those tiny holes in our skin) get clogged with oil, dead skin cells, and bacteria. To keep your pores clear, gently wash your face once or twice a day with warm water and mild soap. And try not to touch your face during the day, especially if you do have a few pimples. Picking at them or squeezing them will just make them worse.

If your face breaks out a lot, ask your mom or dad to help you find the right skincare products.

Tip Clip

Be sure to wear sunscreen when you're outside. Tans and burns aren't healthy. They damage your skin.

Q My best friend is much prettier than I am. Sometimes I'm so jealous! What should I do?

A It's totally natural to compare ourselves to others—we all do it—but that doesn't mean it's good for us! The key is to accept yourself as you are and spend time on the things that make you happy. Don't waste time on things you can't change. Besides, everyone has a different definition of pretty. You think your friend is prettier than you, but someone else might think that YOU are the prettier one. So what does it really matter? Enjoy being best friends, and don't let jealousy get in the way.

Q Some days I hate my nose. Other days I hate my chin or my freckles. I never look in the mirror and like what I see.

A You are way too hard on yourself! That nose of yours? No one else in the world has exactly the same one. It's unique to you. So are your chin and freckles. Be an individual, and own what you have. Being critical about things you can't change won't get you anywhere. It will just get in your way. You are a whole person, not a collection of parts.

It's about being happy with ourselves and trying to make the world a better place.

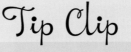

Tip Clip

Being happy is the best beauty treatment ever. People will sense your confidence and be drawn to you.

Q I'm bigger than all my friends. And I don't just mean that I'm taller. What should I do when kids tease me about being overweight? Sometimes even my best friends say things that hurt my feelings.

A People come in all shapes and sizes. Just look around. Let your friends know that you don't judge them by their size, and they shouldn't judge you by yours either. Be clear and direct. Your friends might not realize how hurtful they're being.

What should you do if other kids tease you? Ignore them, change the subject, or leave. If the teasing gets really bad, and they won't stop, tell an adult. That's bullying, and you shouldn't have to deal with bullying by yourself.

Remember, your weight is just one part of you. It's not the whole picture. Be strong, believe in yourself, and be proud of who you are.

Q I need to get braces on my teeth soon. Do braces hurt? I'm kind of freaked out.

A Lots of kids get braces to fix their teeth. No need to freak out. Braces can be a hassle, but you'll get used to them quickly. Your teeth may be sore for a few days right after you get them. Stick with soft foods, like macaroni or yogurt, until they feel better. About once a month, you'll get your braces adjusted. Your teeth may hurt a bit again for a day or so. The orthodontist will answer all of your questions and teach you how to take care of your braces.

Having braces will be worth it in the end. Keep picturing the amazing smile you'll have when the braces come off!

Q A couple of girls in my class told me they're going on a diet. I'm not overweight, but should I go on a diet too?

A Don't fall for all the dieting hype. Kids shouldn't go on diets unless a doctor tells them to. Being healthy is what's important. Right now you're growing the body you'll have for life. So take care of it. Eat fruits, vegetables, whole grains, and lean meats. Drink plenty of water. Try to get about an hour of exercise each day. Walk the dog, bike to your friend's house, or go inline skating with your cousins. If you live in a healthy way, you'll be at the right weight for you.

Q My eye doctor says I need glasses, but I'm scared I won't like the way I look. I want to get contacts but my dads think I'm too young.

A Most kids are nervous about getting their first pair of glasses. It's a big change. Think of shopping for glasses like shopping for another accessory—say, a scarf or earrings. Take your time picking out your frames. Try on different styles and colors. See how they look with your hair and face shape. Glasses can add to your fab style. If possible, get more than one pair, so you can switch off according to your mood.

Contacts take longer to adjust to and are a lot more work, so listen to your dads on that one. If you still want contacts when you're older, you can talk about it then.

Q A few of the girls in my class have started to wear mascara and eye shadow. What's the right age to start wearing makeup?

A That depends on how your parents feel about makeup. Before you buy or start using makeup, talk to them. Everybody's family is different.

Most girls don't start wearing makeup until middle school. Or they wear it for a special occasion, like a dance recital or play. Some girls keep it simple, starting with just a little lip gloss.

There's no rule that says girls or women HAVE to wear makeup. To some people, it feels weird. Others think makeup makes them look more like themselves. Figure out what works best for you. But there's no need to hurry. You've got plenty of time.

Tip Clip

Don't let others push you into shaving, wearing makeup, dressing in a certain way, or anything like that. Your body—your call.

Boys

Q Why do boys in my class act like little kids? Why can't they act their age?

A Girls develop sooner than boys—mentally and physically. So right now the differences between boys and girls can seem huge! Be patient. And remember that growing up is just as awkward and confusing for boys as it is for girls. In time the boys will catch up.

Q A few of the girls in my class have boyfriends. They talk about going on dates and kissing. I've had crushes on boys, but I wouldn't want to kiss them! Is there something wrong with me?

A Lots of girls feel the way you do! Some girls think that having a boyfriend makes them cool. But it's not cool to do anything you're not ready for. Plus, you don't know how much of what they're saying is true. Some or all of it could be made up.

People have different ideas of what it means to date. Some kids go on group dates. Boys and girls will all go together to a movie, a bowling alley, or someplace like that. Many parents want kids to wait to date until they're in high school. Others are OK driving their kids to the movies and letting it be a "date."

When it comes to boyfriends and dating, it doesn't really matter what others do. It's up to you and your family.

Q The boy who moved in next door is super cute! But whenever I see him, I freeze and don't know what to say. What should I do?

A Funny how a super-cute boy can leave you tongue-tied, isn't it? But he's no different from anyone else. How do you usually get to know people? You probably talk about what you like to do. You see if you have things in common and if you enjoy being around each other. Do those same things now.

It's OK to feel nervous. Once you take the first step and start talking to him, you'll feel more confident. If you don't have anything in common, it doesn't matter how cute he is. Friendships and relationships should be based on more than looks.

Tip Clip

Do you sometimes think boys are from a different planet? If you need advice about boys, don't just ask your mom. Include your dad or other male relatives in the conversation. You might learn a lot.

Q I think I should be able to spend my allowance however I want. My parents don't agree. What do you think?

A Every family has different values and rules when it comes to money. Ask your parents what they're worried about. Do they want you to save your money? Do they think you would waste money on things they wouldn't approve of?

See if you can work out a compromise. Maybe you could use part of your allowance the way you want, but let them put the rest in savings. Or you could alternate weeks. Keep talking with your parents, and you'll figure out a solution.

Q My mom wants to pick out all of my clothes. How can I convince her that I'm old enough to choose what I like?

A Tell your mom how you feel. Then find out where she's coming from. Does she really enjoy buying clothes for you? Is she worried about cost? Does she have strong ideas about what's OK and not OK for you to wear? Get it all out in the open.

You'll probably end up meeting somewhere in the middle—at least for now. She'll get to pick out some things, and you'll get to pick out some things. Whatever happens, try to have a good attitude. Shopping will be more fun that way!

Q My parents come into my room whenever they want. That used to be OK with me, but not anymore. How can I tell them that I want my room to feel like MY room?

A Your parents are probably so used to coming into your room that they don't even think about it. Explain that you'd like more privacy. Ask them to knock first, or have certain hours when they know to leave you alone. In return they might ask you to follow certain rules, like bringing your own dirty clothes to the laundry room.

Keep in mind, it is still their house, but together you should be able to figure out a plan that works.

Tip Clip

If you want to experiment with new clothing styles without spending a lot of money, hold a clothing swap with your friends. You'll all get new-to-you things and will have fun too. (Check with your parents first though!)

I have decided I don't want to eat meat anymore. My parents don't think that's healthy. But it's MY body. It should be MY decision.

It IS your body, but you're their kid, and they're responsible for making sure you get everything your body needs to grow. You can be a vegetarian and still be healthy—definitely! But you need to know what you're doing to get enough protein, iron, and other things. To your parents, going vegetarian—especially for just one person in the family—might seem like a lot of work. But you can make it easier for them if you do your research. There are tons of healthy, kid-friendly vegetarian recipes on the Internet. Many of them even include nutrition info. Or you could check out a recipe book at your library.

Are your parents concerned about cost? Pre-packaged vegetarian foods can be pricy. But if you learn to cook with vegetables, beans, rice, and whole grains, eating veggie can be cheaper than eating meat. Pitch in with the planning, cooking, and cleanup, and your parents might start seeing things your way.

I feel like a little kid when my parents hire a babysitter. I'm ready to stay home by myself. Why can't they see that?

Sometimes parents have a hard time seeing that their kids are growing up. They just want to keep their kids safe, at any age, even if it means hiring a babysitter.

If you're serious about staying home alone, talk to your parents. See if you can have a trial run. Ask them to make a list of rules they expect you to follow and phone numbers to call in case of an emergency. If the trial run goes well, your parents might agree that you're ready to stay home alone.

Tip Clip

Don't judge other people's food choices. There are lots of reasons people eat or don't eat certain foods, including health issues or cultural traditions.

Plugged In

Q My friend wants me to go to a PG-13 movie with her. My moms don't want me to see PG-13 movies. Should I tell my friend I don't have permission? Or should I go and not tell my parents?

A Tell your friend you're not allowed to see PG-13 movies. She might be disappointed, but she'll understand. There must be more than one movie that you and your friend would like to see. Find one that your parents are OK with.

It can feel really unfair when other kids get to do things you're not allowed to. Just remember that your moms have good reasons for their rules. They know you and what you're ready for.

This movie has been rated

Parental Guidance
PARENTAL GUIDANCE SUGGESTED

some components may not be suitable for children

Q Why do I need a parent's permission to join a social media site? If the site's for kids, why can't I just sign up by myself?

A The Internet is like its own universe. It's enormous! And it's easy to stumble onto things you wish you'd never seen or to be tricked into giving private information. Parents need to see for themselves that the sites you're going to are safe and at the right age level. The people who make social media sites for kids understand that. They want parents to trust them. Without that trust, the site wouldn't be able to exist. Sure, it's a little annoying to have to get your parents involved. But it's just to keep you safe.

Tip Clip

Online manners count! Don't say anything online that you wouldn't say in person.

Q What's wrong with having a computer or TV in my room? My parents won't let me have either one, and I don't think that's fair.

A There are lots of things on TV and the Internet that aren't kid-friendly. If TVs and computers are in a family area, it's easier for your parents to see what you're watching and make sure the programs are right for you.

It's easy to lose track of time when you're surfing the web or watching TV. Too much screen time isn't good for your brain or your body. Did you know you're supposed to stop your screen time at least an hour before going to bed? You'll sleep better if you do. Your parents' rule might not seem fair, but they're doing what they think is best for you.

Q My dad turns off the radio in the car when certain songs are on. I get annoyed, but he says some songs are bad. What can be so bad about a song on the radio?

A Movies have ratings that tell you if a movie is OK for kids. Think of your dad like a ratings monitor for songs on the radio. He knows that some songs have language or ideas he doesn't think you're old enough for yet. Your dad's just watching out for you and trying to do what's right. Maybe you could work together to make a playlist that everyone in your family would enjoy.

Q Some of my friends have cell phones. My parents say I'm too young. What can I say to convince them I'm old enough?

A There's not much you can SAY, but there's plenty you can DO. Keep track of your things, help around the house without being asked, and follow the house rules. A cell phone is a big deal. It costs a lot of money. Your parents may worry that you'll lose it, break it, or run up a huge phone bill. Even if you do everything right, they might still say no. But if you earn their trust, they'll be more likely to say yes.

Tip Clip

It's good to unplug every so often. Spend a few days without your computer or tablet. Who knows what adventures you'll have!

Glossary

accessory—something that goes with your clothes, such as a belt or jewelry

bacteria—very small living things that exist all around you and inside you; some bacteria cause disease, but most don't

bullying—being mean and hurtful to another person on purpose, again and again

compromise—an agreement in which each side gives up part of its demands

convince—to cause a person to believe or do something

embarrassed—feeling shame

gland—an organ in the body that makes certain chemicals; sweat, tears, and hormones are released by glands

growth spurt—a short period of time during which a child grows a lot

hormone—a chemical made by a gland in the body that affects growth and development

privacy—space belonging to one person or group and no one else

puberty—the time when a person's body changes from a child's to an adult's

pubic—relating to the area near the genitals

relationship—the connection between people; the way they get along

responsible—able to be trusted to do what you say you will do

social media—electronic communication through which large groups of people share ideas with one another

tease—to make fun of someone

value—a belief or idea that is important to a person

vegetarian—someone who does not eat meat

Read More

Katz, Anne, and Monika Melnychuk. *Girl in the Know: Your Inside-and-Out Guide to Growing up.* Toronto: Kids Can, 2010.

McGuinness, Lisa, and Chris Boral. *Gotcha Covered!: Everything You Need to Know About Your Period.* San Francisco: Chronicle, 2008.

Vermond, Kira, and Carl Chin. *Growing Up: Inside and Out.* Toronto: Owlkids, 2013.

Internet Sites

FactHound offers a safe, fun way to find Internet sites related to this book. All of the sites on FactHound have been researched by our staff.

Here's all you do:

Visit www.facthound.com

Type in this code: 9781491418604

 Check out projects, games and lots more at
www.capstonekids.com

Index

For my parents—NL

For my daughter, Lydia, the most courageous girl I'll ever know—PS

Snap Books are published by Capstone Press,
1710 Roe Crest Drive, North Mankato, Minnesota 56003
www.capstonepub.com

Library of Congress Cataloging-in-Publication Data
Loewen, Nancy, 1964–
 Tangles, growth spurts, and being you : questions and answers about growing up / by Nancy Loewen and Paula Skelley ; illustrated by Julissa Mora.
     pages cm.—(Snap books. Girl talk)
 Includes index.
 Summary: "Provides tween-girl-specific information about growing up in a question-answer format"—Provided by publisher.
 ISBN 978-1-4914-1860-4 (library binding)
 ISBN 978-1-4914-1865-9 (eBook PDF)
1. Teenage girls—Physiology—Juvenile literature. 2. Teenage girls—Social conditions—Juvenile literature. 3. Preteens—Physiology—Juvenile literature. 4. Preteens—Social conditions—Juvenile literature. 5. Puberty—Juvenile literature. 6. Child development—Juvenile literature. I. Skelley, Paula. II. Mora, Julissa, illustrator. III. Title.
 RJ144.L64 2015
 613'.04243—dc23   2014027732

Editorial Credits
Jill Kalz, editor; Juliette Peters, designer; Svetlana Zhurkin, media researcher; Charmaine Whitman, production specialist

Photo Credits
Getty Images: Jose Luis Pelaez Inc, 27, SW Productions, 13; iStockphotos: kali9, 18, LL28, 24, monkeybusinessimages, 20; Shutterstock: Andy Dean Photography, 21, bikeriderlondon, 23, Blend Images, 8, Dragon Images, 28, Elena Elisseeva, cover, 11, glenda, 6, michaeljung, 15, Pinkcandy, 10, rangizzz, 17, Smiltena, 12

About the Consultant

John E. Desrochers, PhD, is a licensed psychologist and certified school psychologist who has worked for more than 30 years with children and families in schools, clinics, and private practice. He earned his doctorate in educational psychology at Columbia University and also holds graduate degrees in remedial reading, behavior analysis, and marriage and family therapy. John has numerous professional publications and was recognized with a School Psychologist of the Year Award by the National Association of School Psychologists.

Look for all the books in the series:

About the Authors

Nancy Loewen has published many books for kids. She's a two-time Minnesota Book Award finalist (*Four to the Pole* and *The LAST Day of Kindergarten*) and the recipient of a Distinguished Achievement Award from the Association of Educational Publishers (Writer's Toolbox series). She holds an MFA from Hamline University in St. Paul. Nancy has two children and lives near Minneapolis. To learn more, visit *www.nancyloewen.com*.

Paula Skelley is a blogger who writes about life, loss, and pediatric cancer awareness. She holds a BS in English and sociology and an MA in English (creative writing concentration) from Minnesota State University, Mankato. She is a mother of two and lives in the New Hampshire Seacoast Region.

Nancy and Paula met years ago as English majors at MSU, Mankato, and they have been friends ever since. This is their first project together.